W9-BPP-485

Leeches

Leeches

Patrick Merrick

THE CHILD'S WORLD®, INC.

Library of Congress Cataloging-in-Publication Data
Merrick, Patrick.
Leeches / by Patrick Merrick.
p.   cm.
Includes index.
Summary: Describes the physical characteristics, behavior,
and habitat of leeches—slimy, worm-like creatures.
ISBN 1-56766-633-7 (lib. reinforced : alk. paper)
1. Leeches—Juvenile literature.
[1. Leeches.]   I. Title.
QL391.A6M476   1999
592'.66—dc21   98-44320
CIP
AC

Photo Credits

ANIMALS ANIMALS © Breck P. Kent: 30
ANIMALS ANIMALS © Oxford Scientific Films: 15
ANIMALS ANIMALS © Robert Maier: 2
© Bill Beatty/Visuals Unlimited: 26
© David Liebman: 6
© Dwight R. Kuhn: 24
© 1999 E.R. Degginger/Dembinsky Photo Assoc. Inc.: 13, 16, 23
© 1999 Larry Mishkar/Dembinsky Photo Assoc. Inc.: 9
© Robert and Linda Mitchell: cover, 10, 19, 20, 29

On the cover...

Front cover: This leech is feeding on a person in Malaysia.
Page 2: This *medicinal leech* is swimming in a tank in Germany.

Table of Contents

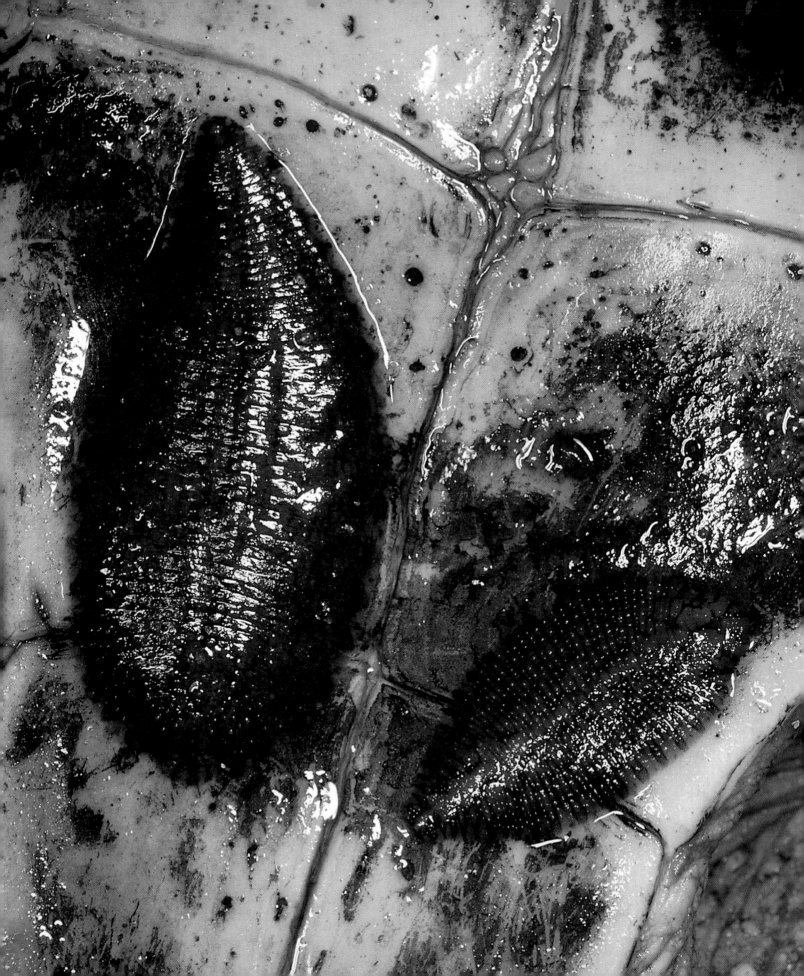

With the summer sun high in the sky, it's a great day to go to the lake. As you sit near the shore, you notice a little turtle resting in the warm water. You walk over to the turtle and look at its beautiful colors. As you look more closely, you see that something is attached to the turtle. It's a small, slimy creature—and it's drinking the turtle's blood! What type of animal is this? It's a leech.

⇐ These *turtle leeches* are feeding on a snapping turtle.

Where Do Leeches Live?

There are more than 300 kinds, or **species,** of leeches. Most leech species live in lakes or ponds. That's because they like warm, slow-moving water. Others live in the ocean. Some live on land in very damp plants or dirt.

Leeches can even live in places that get cold or have long dry spells. If the water dries up or gets too cold, the leeches can dig into the mud and sleep for months. When the water is right again, the leeches come out and begin looking for food.

This *freshwater leech* is swimming on the bottom of a lake. ⇒

What Do Leeches Look Like?

When you first see a leech, it might look like an earthworm you would find in your garden. That's because leeches are related to worms. Like a worm, a leech is really just a stomach inside a soft, tube-like body. A leech's body is divided into 34 sections or **annuli.** Leeches' bodies can be very colorful. There are black, gray, red, orange, and even spotted leeches. Leeches are usually very small, but some can grow to be 18 inches long.

⇐ It's easy to see the annuli on this leech as it crawls along.

A leech does not have a nose, ears, or even eyes. What it does have, however, are two suckers. The front of the leech has a small sucker, and the back has a larger one.

If you touch a leech, you will feel that it is slimy. The slime has a very important job—it lets the leech breathe. Unlike people, leeches do not have lungs. Instead, the leech breathes with its whole body. The air soaks into the slime on the leech's skin. Without the slime, a leech's body would dry out, and the leech would die.

The head of this *pond leech* is near the bottom of the page. ⇒

How Are Baby Leeches Born?

Unlike most other animals, a leech is both a male and a female. When two leeches mate, both of them lay eggs. Some leeches make protective coverings called **cocoons** and place their eggs inside. Other species simply drop their eggs in the water or attach them to plants. Some leeches even carry their eggs around with them! After a few weeks, the tiny eggs hatch, and new, fully formed leeches are born.

This leech is keeping its young safe on its belly. ⇒

How Do Leeches Find Food?

Since leeches cannot see or hear, they must use other ways to find their food, or **prey.** Leeches have a very good sense of smell. One of their favorite smells is blood. In fact, whenever leeches smell blood, they swim quickly toward whatever is bleeding.

Leeches are also very sensitive to movement. When an animal walks on the ground or swims through the water, it causes tiny movements. The movements are called **vibrations.** Leeches feel these vibrations and move toward them. They want to see if they can eat whatever is moving!

⇐ This leech is swimming toward its next meal.

How Do Leeches Move?

Since leeches do not have any legs or feet, you might wonder how they move. On land, a leech uses its suckers to help it move. It sticks down one sucker and then loops its body up and over. The suckers help the leech to "walk." In the water, leeches move about easily by swimming.

This leech is crawling along the floor of a rain forest in Malaysia. ⇒

What Do Leeches Eat?

Different kinds of leeches eat different things. Some eat snails, worms, or other leeches. Most, however, are known for eating something else—blood! Leeches feed on the blood of fish, turtles, birds, frogs, and even people.

When a leech finds its prey, it uses its back sucker to attach itself to the animal. Then it uses its front sucker to chew a small opening in the animal's skin. When the opening is big enough, the leech starts to feed. A leech can drink more than five times its weight in blood in one feeding. That would be like eating 1,000 hamburgers at one time! Since leeches eat so much at one time, they can go several months between feedings.

⇐ This leech is feeding on the photographer's arm.

It might seem like leeches would hurt their prey by drinking so much blood. That does not happen. Since leeches are so small, most of the time the animal doesn't even know the leech is there! The leech takes some of the animal's blood, but not enough to hurt the animal. Once the leech is done feeding, it simply falls off the animal.

This fat pond leech has finished its meal and is resting on a rock. ⇒

Leeches have lots of enemies. Turtles, frogs, and birds all like to eat leeches when they can find them. One of the biggest enemies to leeches is fish. In fact, so many fish like to eat leeches, fisherman often use leeches as bait!

⇐ This snapping turtle has caught a leech for lunch.

Since leeches drink blood, they sometimes attach themselves to people. Even so, they are not dangerous. If you find a leech on you, sprinkle some salt on it. The leech will soon release its suckers and stop feeding. Then it will fall off and leave you alone. Never pull a leech off when it is attached to your skin. Parts of its suckers might stay on your body and cause an infection.

⇐ Here a leech is crawling slowly across a man's hand.

Are Leeches Helpful?

Some doctors have learned that leeches can actually help people by sucking their blood. Sometimes when people have surgery, their wounds swell up and hurt. Sticking leeches on the wounds to suck out the extra blood helps the patients heal faster. As the leeches suck, they also release special chemicals into the person's body that helps the person heal. Years ago in France, leeches were raised on special farms to be used for this purpose. Today, however, leech farms are not common.

Doctors sometimes use medicinal leeches like this one. ⇒

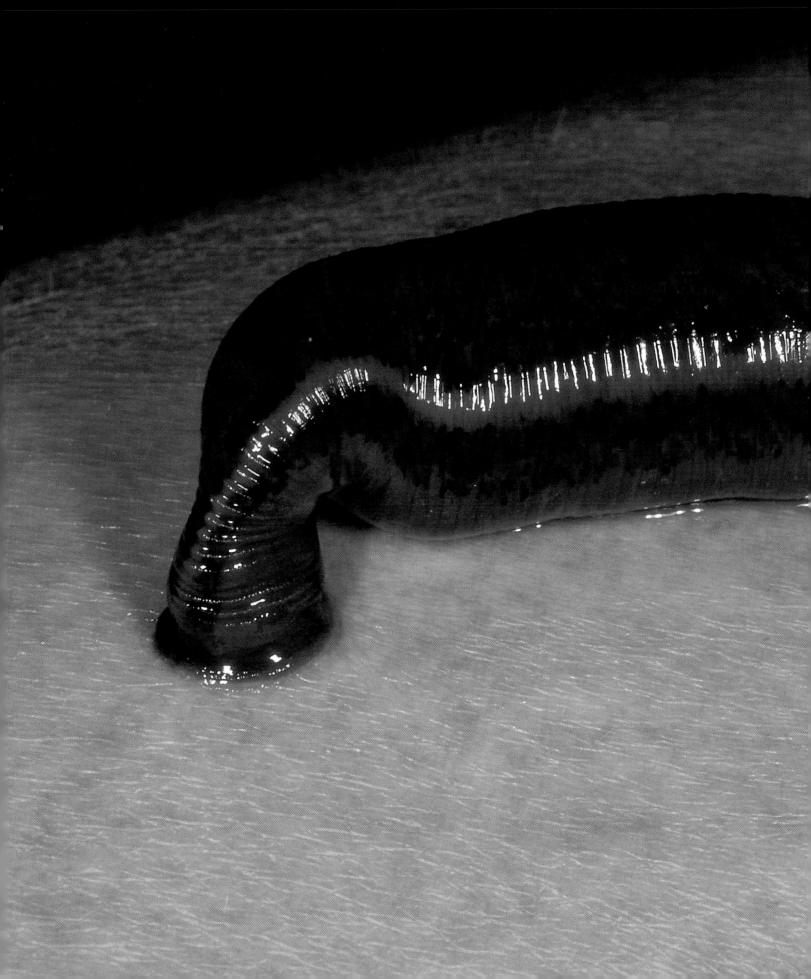

So, even though leeches might look slimy or yucky, they can actually be helpful. And even though they eat blood, they are not bad or mean animals. They are just trying to stay alive and raise their babies. The next time you see a leech swimming along, take a closer look. Instead of being afraid of it, think of all the interesting things it can do!

Glossary

annuli (ANN–yuh–lee)
Annuli are the narrow sections that make up a leech's body. The sections are easy to see.

cocoons (kuh–KOONZ)
Cocoons are covers some animals make to protect their young. Some leeches make cocoons to protect their eggs.

prey (PRAY)
An animal that other animals hunt and eat for food is called prey. Turtles, fish, birds, and people are all prey for leeches.

species (SPEE–sheez)
A species is a different kind of an animal. There are more than 300 species of leeches.

vibrations (vy–BRAY–shunz)
Vibrations are movements. Leeches feel vibrations and track them down to find their food.

Index

Web Sites

Learn more about leeches:

http://www.accessexcellence.org/LC/SS/leechlove.html

http://www.alienexplorer.com/ecology/topic18.html

http://animaldiversity.ummz.umich.edu/annelida.html